My South Sea Adventure

Jungle Islands

by Maria Coffey with Debora Pearson

Photography by Dag Goering

Maria (right) and Dag (left) in the Solomon Islands

Annick Press ◆ Toronto ◆ New York ◆ Vancouver

Wagina Island

Kukutin

Kia

New Georgia Sound

Kora Island

Kolumbangara
Island

Vonavona
Island

Noro
Munda

New Georgia
Island

Marovo
Lagoon

Skull Island

Chubikopi

Njapuana
Island

Baraula Village

Vangunu
Island

Mbili
Village

Roviana Lagoon

Nusa Hope

Minjanga
Island

N

W   E

S

Map is not to scale

Litogharira

Santa Isabel Island

Kilokaka

Kaevanga

Solomon Islands

Australia

South
Pacific
Ocean

New Zealand

Honiara

Guadalcanal

Help!
I'm Drowning!

I've paddled a kayak down the River Ganges in India and up Lake Malawi in Africa. I have been over the Sea of Cortez in Mexico, along the Danube River in Europe, and through the Solomon Sea in the South Pacific Ocean. During my long-distance travels, I've crossed shark-filled waters, faced river bandits, and come face-to-face with wild hippos.

I've had many exciting adventures while paddling a kayak and today I can't imagine life away from the water. But it wasn't always that way for me. Many years ago, long before I ever stepped into a kayak, I almost drowned.

That experience scared me so badly that all I could think was, *"I am never going in open water again."* Swimming, kayaking – anything to do with being in or around water – were the last things I ever wanted to do.

My terrifying experience happened without warning. I was off the coast of Morocco in Africa, playing in the ocean with some other people. I wasn't a strong swimmer and so I didn't take chances – I stayed where the water came up only to my chest. It made me feel safe knowing I could touch the ground beneath my feet and see the shore close by.

Suddenly, a big wave rolled in and broke over my head. It knocked me off my feet, then the undertow sucked me into deep water. I shouted to a woman on shore for help. Unable to believe her eyes, she simply stared at me and stood there as the water pulled me away.

I tried to swim to safety but the water

After almost drowning, I was terrified of open water. But I finally overcame my fear.

yanked me back. Again and again I tried, but I just could not break free. Within moments, I was so far out that the people on shore looked tiny, unreal. Rough waves slapped my face. Water poured in my mouth and I choked. I began to panic.

I saw waves breaking over some rocks and suddenly I imagined myself being smashed against them, and killed. As I slipped under again, a fierce thought hit me: *"I don't want to die!"* I sputtered to the surface and kept on fighting.

After a time, the current swept me toward the shore, far from where I had started out. There, a man saw my body in the surf. Aware of the undertow, and the danger, he ran into the water, grabbed me by the hair and dragged me onto the beach. I felt myself being pulled through the water, the surf rushing past …

Later, I learned that this place was well-known for its treacherous currents. Over the years, many local fishermen had been swept away. None had survived. I didn't know this at the time. All I knew, after I came to, was that I was back on land. My awful experience was over.

But the memory of it stayed and left me with a deep fear of water. Never, I vowed, would I go into open water again. It would be many years before I had any reason to change my mind.

There are hundreds and hundreds of islands that make up the Solomons. Some islands are so tiny that they can only hold one or two palm trees. On big islands, you'll find mountains carpeted with jungle, and villages too.

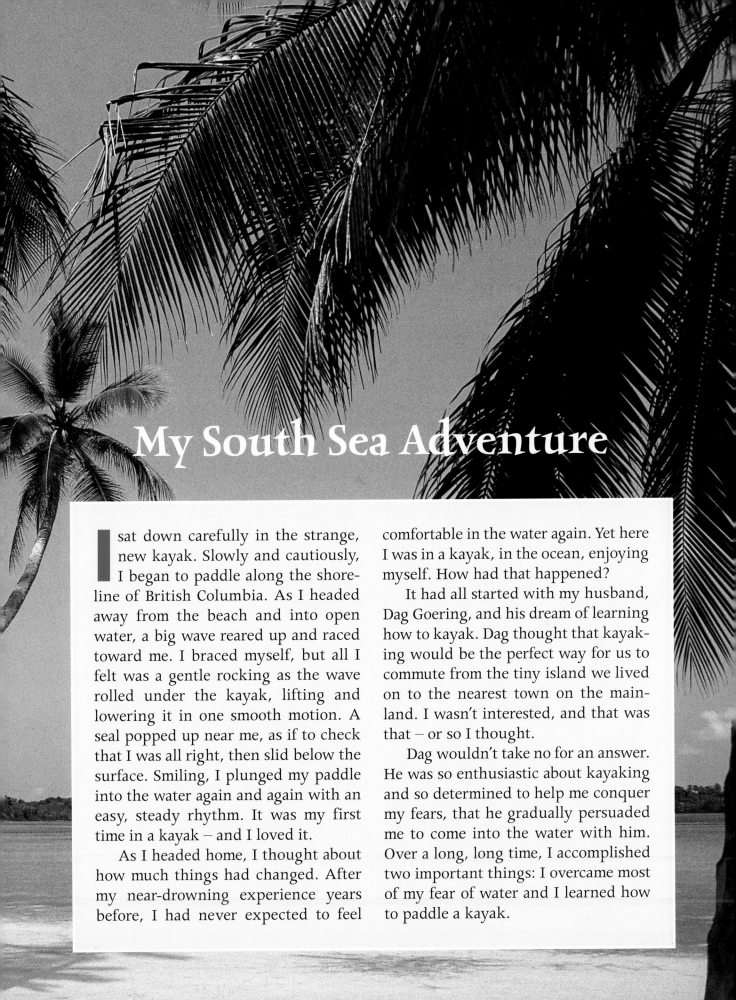

My South Sea Adventure

I sat down carefully in the strange, new kayak. Slowly and cautiously, I began to paddle along the shoreline of British Columbia. As I headed away from the beach and into open water, a big wave reared up and raced toward me. I braced myself, but all I felt was a gentle rocking as the wave rolled under the kayak, lifting and lowering it in one smooth motion. A seal popped up near me, as if to check that I was all right, then slid below the surface. Smiling, I plunged my paddle into the water again and again with an easy, steady rhythm. It was my first time in a kayak – and I loved it.

As I headed home, I thought about how much things had changed. After my near-drowning experience years before, I had never expected to feel comfortable in the water again. Yet here I was in a kayak, in the ocean, enjoying myself. How had that happened?

It had all started with my husband, Dag Goering, and his dream of learning how to kayak. Dag thought that kayaking would be the perfect way for us to commute from the tiny island we lived on to the nearest town on the mainland. I wasn't interested, and that was that – or so I thought.

Dag wouldn't take no for an answer. He was so enthusiastic about kayaking and so determined to help me conquer my fears, that he gradually persuaded me to come into the water with him. Over a long, long time, I accomplished two important things: I overcame most of my fear of water and I learned how to paddle a kayak.

At first, kayaking was simply a way to carry things we bought in town, across the water, to our home. But we quickly discovered that kayaking was the perfect way to go almost anywhere we wanted along the coast. Because a kayak needs very little water to float in, we could take it to beaches and shallow bays that other boats couldn't reach. In a kayak, we could carry enough food and supplies for trips that lasted weeks at a time. And because we travelled slowly in a kayak, there was always lots of time to enjoy the scenery and watch the wildlife around us.

We paddled among the islands near our home, then we began exploring the coast of British Columbia. The more places we saw, the more we wanted to see. Most of all, we hoped to visit some remote, unknown parts of the world and take our kayak with us.

The Solomon Islands, in the South Pacific Ocean, were both far-off and unfamiliar. The first time I heard about these islands, I had to look them up on a map just to see where they were. Few people had been to the Solomons and hardly anyone had written about that part of the world. The little information that we found made me curious to learn more – and filled me with fear.

According to what Dag and I read, the waters around the Solomon Islands were filled with man-eating sharks, making it one of the worst places in the world for shark attacks. The Solomons were also one of the worst places for getting malaria, an often-deadly disease spread by some mosquitoes. At one time, head-hunting people lived there. Giant centipedes still lived there. Worst of all for me, the Solomons were home to saltwater crocodiles – and I've been afraid of crocodiles all my life.

In spite of these dangers, I was also drawn to this strange part of the world. The Solomons had lush jungles and, ever since I was little, I had dreamed of exploring a jungle. The jungles in the Solomon Islands had lovely cockatoos, fragrant orchid plants that grew waist-high, and birdwing butterflies the size of a man's hand. What would it be like to see all of that and more?

My dream was about to come true. "Let's do it!" said Dag one evening, as we paddled around our island. "Let's fly to the South Pacific and kayak around the Solomon Islands. It will be an adventure, Maria!"

I couldn't help laughing. Paddling a kayak in the Solomon Islands would be an adventure, perhaps *the* adventure of a lifetime. It would be our chance to explore a part of the world most people would never see. I took a deep breath and tried to forget about the sharks, the malaria, the centipedes, and especially the crocodiles …

"All right," I replied, dipping my paddle in the water. "We'll go to the Solomon Islands!"

Maria Coffey

Different kinds of orchids grow all over the Solomons. Some of them have the most beautiful perfume you can imagine – it's so powerful that you can smell orchids before you're close enough to see them.

Where Am I Now?

In Honiara, the capital city of the Solomon Islands, we boarded an old ferry to Mbili. As we pulled away from the dock, I peeked into the engine room: oily pistons pounded away and heat poured out ...

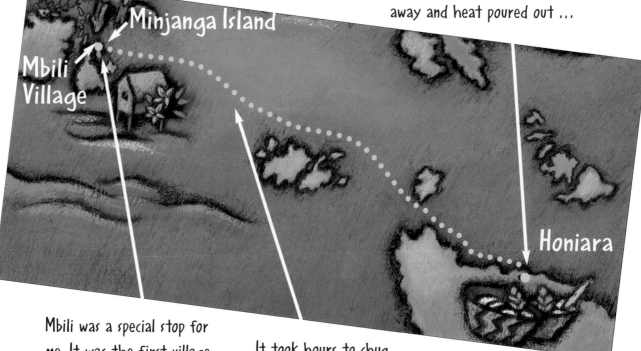

Minjanga Island

Mbili Village

Honiara

Mbili was a special stop for me. It was the first village we stayed at in the Solomons — and the first place I saw a child-sized dugout canoe.

It took hours to chug our way to Mbili. By the time we drew close, it was midnight. Most of the other passengers were asleep, but not me. I was too excited!

Chapter 1

All Aboard!

Our kayak is folded up in the red sack. I was eager to unpack it and start paddling.

"Your boat is in that bag?" asked the stranger with disbelief, looking at me, then at Dag.

He pointed across the crowded ferry boat to the red sack containing our folded-up kayak. It lay next to a teetering pile of cardboard boxes, a grunting pig in a snug cloth bag, and some heavy sacks of rice. Dag and I had boarded the ferry in Honiara, the capital city of the Solomon Islands, and were on our way to the village of Mbili on Minjanga Island. From there, I explained to the stranger, we would begin to explore Marovo Lagoon, and beyond, by kayak.

The stranger moved aside to let another stream of passengers squeeze past, then spoke again. "And you are going to paddle this … kayak? … all around the islands?" He shook his head again. Clearly, he had never met anyone or heard of anyone who had done such a peculiar thing.

As the ferry pulled away from the wharf, I listened to some women speaking Pidgin English, the common language used in the Solomons. I looked at the men whose mouths were stained red from chewing betel nuts and lime. Some of them had faces that were scarred with traditional tattoos. The stranger, whose name was Jim, wasn't the only one who could scarcely believe that we would soon be paddling around the Solomons – I could hardly believe it myself. It still seemed incredible to me that we were here in the Solomons, about to begin our kayaking adventure.

"After the ferry drops us at Minjanga Island," I told Jim, "we'll camp for the night. In the morning, we'll assemble the kayak and load our supplies in it. Then we will begin paddling."

"Did someone from Mbili invite you to stay with them?" he asked. Jim, it turned out, was a retired schoolteacher who made his home in that village.

Dag and I glanced at each other, then back at Jim. No one had invited us, but that wasn't a problem … or was it?

"The ferry stops near Mbili after dark, around midnight," Jim told us. "Nighttime in the Solomons is when many spirits come out. Fearful things can happen. That is what people here believe."

It was a long, hot ferry ride to Mbili but I didn't really notice. We were here, in the Solomons!

Our food basket had a banana leaf "parcel" with steamed pork and vegetable roots in it.

Jim continued, "If the people of Mbili see you, two strangers after dark, they will think you are evil spirits. I will tell them that you are my friends from far away and that I have invited you to stay with me. Then others will not be afraid of you."

Gratefully, we accepted Jim's offer and invited him to share a basket of food we had purchased earlier. The ferry chugged steadily along. Many hours later, around midnight, it slowed down.

"We are almost at Minjanga Island and the village of Mbili," announced Jim.

I stepped over a family sleeping soundly on their floor mats and peered over the railing into the deep black. There were no lights, no signs of a village anywhere. Where exactly, I wondered, *was* Mbili?

Two motorized dugouts, long boats made from hollowed-out logs with engines on the back, suddenly appeared by the ferry. Dag and I followed Jim into one

Lights Out!

If you visit the Solomons, you'll notice that the sun sets early here. Around 7:00 pm, it's so dark that you need lights to see. If you're in a large town, such as Honiara or Noro, you can simply switch on a light. In these towns, electricity is produced in a central power station. It's distributed throughout the town and used to power everything from radios and refrigerators to desk lamps and streetlights.

Villages are smaller than towns and don't have central sources of electrical power. Some people in villages buy their own little power stations, called generators, and use them to run their lights, freezers, videocassette recorders, and other electrical equipment. People who don't have generators use lamps that burn kerosene fuel.

Just like kids anywhere, kids in the Solomon Islands love making music and listening to it. One time I heard Madonna singing on a radio.

dugout, and watched as our kayak and bags were loaded into another one. We left the brightly lit ferry behind and threaded our way through the dark to Mbili.

As our dugouts scraped the beach, I smelled the scent of frangipani flowers. We grabbed our bags, then followed Jim along a tree-lined trail to his house. It stood on long, wooden legs. Near the stilts, a dog chewed on a coconut shell. Inside the house, Jim's wife, Linethy, showed us to our bed, a floor mat in the main room.

I was exhausted and gratefully lay down. When I did, I made a surprising discovery. I had expected that nights in the Solomon Islands would be very quiet and peaceful. But, on this night at least, there was lots of noise. Mosquitoes buzzed and droned in our ears. Cats snarled and brawled nearby. Somewhere a baby cried. And through it all, the dog gnawed on the coconut shell as if it were a juicy bone. We were out in the middle of the South Pacific and it was too noisy to sleep!

As daylight poured into our room, one of Jim's daughters walked in. She stared at

The kids I met were shy at first because they hadn't seen many visitors like me before. But it didn't take long before they began asking me questions and showing me around.

What Did You Say?

These kids helped teach me Pidgin English – and they only laughed a little at my mistakes!

There are over 80 different languages spoken throughout the Solomon Islands. However, you don't need to learn all of these languages to talk to someone here – all you need to know is a little Pidgin English. It contains some English words and it's the one language used almost everywhere in the Solomons. Here are three words that are good to know if you meet someone who speaks Pidgin English:

Kastom ("CUS-tem"):

This Pidgin English word has a similar meaning to the English word "custom" – it means something that has been done a certain way for generations and generations. Respecting "kastom" beliefs and ways of life is important in the Solomons. Going against "kastom" is known as "tambu".

Wantok ("WAHN-talk"):

A "wantok" is usually a relative, someone who is from the same family as you. Sometimes a "wantok" can be a close friend. It is "kastom" to share your home, food, and belongings with your "wantoks": if they turn up at your home, you must take care of them.

Tambu ("Tam-BOO"):

This word means "forbidden" or "not allowed". For example, refusing to help members of your family is "tambu" in the Solomon Islands.

us, then fled from the room, sobbing and shrieking. I heard Linethy comforting her.

"It's a good thing she didn't run into us last night," yawned Dag, sitting up on the mat. "Can you imagine what she would have thought if she'd seen us then?"

By the time we had settled down to have breakfast with Jim and Linethy, Jim's daughter had forgotten her fears. While we dined on freshly-picked pawpaw fruit, watermelon, and coconut biscuits we'd brought with us from Honiara, she quietly tiptoed over to us, followed by some of her friends. They sat together on the ground watching everything Dag and I did – from sipping water to breaking off a piece of biscuit – with great curiosity, as though they'd never seen anyone do these things before. I smiled at them and they broke into soft, shy giggles.

While Dag pulled out our map to show Jim our travel route, I gazed beyond the village houses to the jungle. Much of the land on Minjanga Island looked wild and unclaimed: it appeared that no one owned any of it. That's what I thought, but I was wrong. The land did belong to someone.

Jim told us that almost all the land in the

Coconuts: The Inside Story

A hard-shelled coconut is not only the fruit of the coconut palm tree – it's also the giant seed from which a new tree sprouts. Years from now, when this tree is fully grown, it will be taller than a four-storey building and bear its own seeds.

Solomons, and all the water immediately around it, is owned by someone. Before camping out or fishing anywhere, we would have to find the landowner and get their permission. We would also be expected to offer them a gift, called "compensation," in return for their hospitality.

Luckily for us, Jim owned some of the land where we were going. "This belongs to me," he said, pointing to some of the land and water marked on our map. "You can stay anywhere, without charge."

Dag and I were eager to begin paddling, so after breakfast we assembled our kayak. After the kayak was in one piece, we carefully packed our bags inside it.

Finally we were ready for the last stage: protecting ourselves from the sun's harsh rays. Without wide-brimmed hats, sunglasses, and sunscreen on our bare skin, we wouldn't last long in the direct sun. As we rubbed on sunscreen, some of the villagers began to laugh and whisper to each other. Others looked at us with pity. I adjusted my sunglasses and turned to Jim.

He spoke to the villagers, then to me.

People from the Solomons stared when they saw me applying sunscreen. They never use it. And they rarely wear sunglasses or sun hats.

Eating sugar cane takes some practice, but it's worth it. First you use your teeth to rip off the tough, outer part of the stalk. Then you bite into it, chew, and suck out the refreshing juice.

"They don't believe me when I tell them that you must do these curious things to protect yourself from the sun."

As we paddled away, I turned back to look at the villagers on the shore. I was sure they were still talking about us and the unusual things we'd done. Our short time on Minjanga Island had reminded me of one important thing: our customs and way of life were just as foreign to these people as their ways were to us.

Already, we were learning new things in this place. I pulled down my hat brim and began paddling into Marovo Lagoon.

When it comes to having fun in the water and exploring the jungle, kids who live in the Solomons are experts. Kids here learn how to paddle a dugout and swim almost before they learn how to walk (see left). By the time they're running and climbing, these kids know which creatures and plants are safe to touch and which ones are dangerous. On the beach and by the water, they watch out for deadly stonefish, and shrimp with sharp, cutting barbs. In the jungle, they avoid poisonous spiders and plant leaves that cause rashes if you brush against them. Kids also know about a tropical plant that makes a handy sweet snack: sugar cane (see above).

Who Owns Land in the Solomons?

Being a landowner in the Solomons means having a place where you can build your house, grow your own food, and earn a living. Owning land here is important, just as it is in most parts of the world. That's why almost all the land here – from the tiniest island to the biggest mangrove swamp – belongs to someone, even though the land may look wild and unclaimed.

The most important landowners are called the custom owners. Custom owners are the people who have inherited land that has been in their family or clan for many generations. (The custom owners also inherit the water that is immediately around the land.) Others may use the land of the custom owners, but only if the custom owners have given them permission to do so. In parts of the Solomons, only women can inherit land. Men are not custom owners in those regions.

Today, some of the "rules" and traditions to do with land ownership are changing. Some land has been divided up and is now owned by individuals, not families.

High in the trees, parrots stared down at me. Spooky growls and spine-tingling screeches rose from a tangle of vines. This was the jungle I had always dreamed of.

Chapter 2

Jungle Eyes

The big, black creature rose out of the treetops and slowly flapped toward us. As it flew overhead, I could see dark skin stretched like a cape across its wings. Each outstretched wing was the length of my arm. There was something about this visitor that made me feel small and exposed – perhaps it was the way it circled over our kayak, again and again. What was it looking for, and what was it going to do next?

"Looks like Dracula has come to pay us a visit," said Dag, squinting up at the sky. "It's just a big bat that eats fruit, not people in kayaks."

As if the bat had heard Dag, it circled one last time, then winged its way back to the jungle. Meanwhile we drew closer to the tiny island where it lived.

The jungle there was like the one I'd always dreamed of. There were vines strong enough for me to swing on, hanging from gnarled tree trunks. I gazed at plants with thick, fleshy leaves bigger than bicycle wheels. Brightly-coloured parrots chattered overhead. Below them,

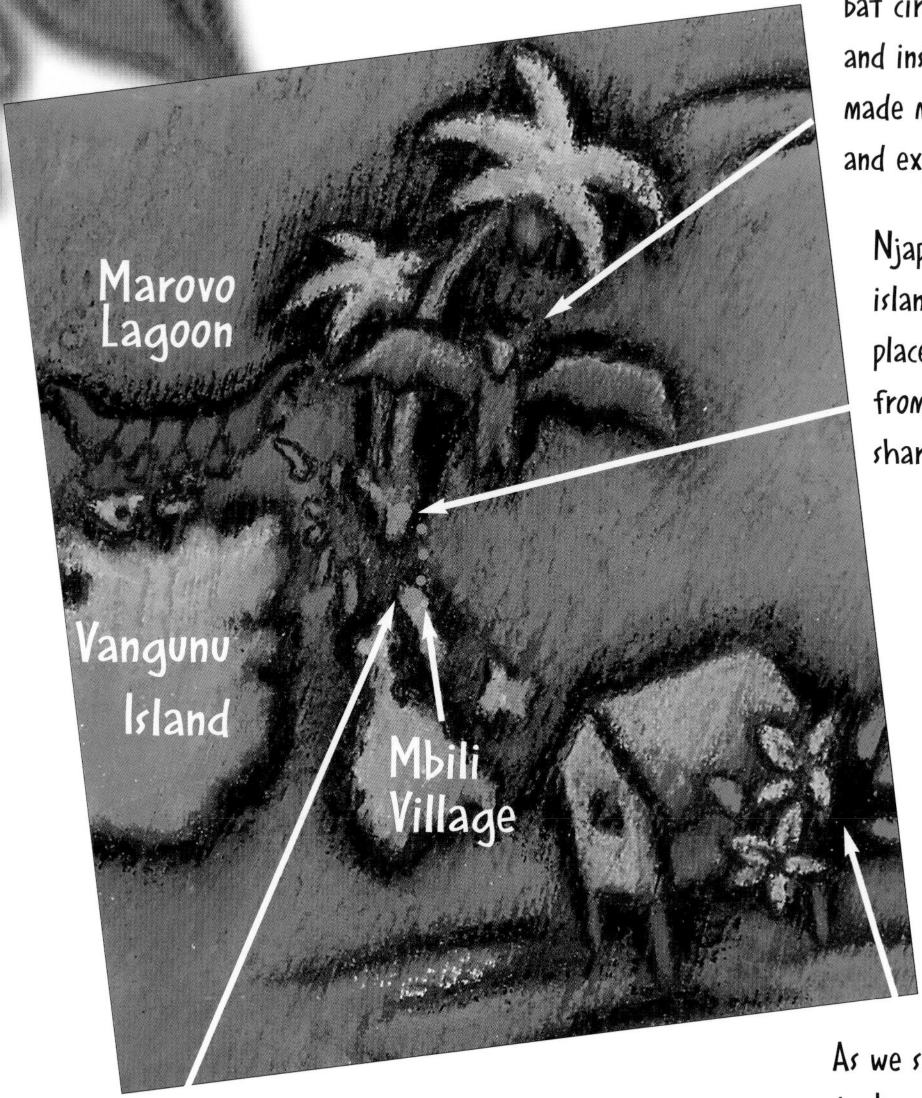

A big, black fruit bat circled overhead and inspected us. It made me feel small and exposed ...

Njapuana was a beautiful island — and a dangerous place. Coconuts shot down from palm trees and reef sharks patrolled the shore.

Marovo Lagoon

Vangunu Island

Mbili Village

Seeing the jungle here was a dream come true for me. Luckily, I didn't spot any crocodiles by the shore — that would have been my worst nightmare!

As we said goodbye to Jim and paddled away from his village, I breathed in the strong sweet smell of frangipani flowers.

Big-Eyed Bat Facts

It has a fox's head, flies like a bird, and it eats fruit. What is this strange creature? It's a "flying fox", or "fruit bat", and it's found in tropical places. All bats, including fruit bats, are mammals and are active at night. Many bats have poor eyesight and must send out sound waves to help them find their way in the dark. The sound waves bounce off objects, telling the bats where things are. But fruit bats don't depend on sound waves – they have big eyes and can see well at night.

a huge butterfly shimmered past, showing off brilliant blue wings as delicate as flower petals. In spite of the weird screeches and spooky growls that came from the dark undergrowth, I wasn't afraid. I stared at the yellow tail feathers of a white cockatoo as it soared by. I was here in the jungle and that was all that mattered!

I was just about to reach out and touch the arching, above-ground roots of a mangrove tree when I remembered something. Mangrove trees grew on the island coasts, in and near the water. They were a gathering place for mudskippers, fish, and lizards. That meant that these trees were also a good place for …

"Crocodiles!" I said to Dag, snatching back my hand. "There are probably lots of crocodiles here!"

Dag didn't look worried. "I asked Jim and he said there weren't any crocodiles in Marovo Lagoon. They were all hunted some time ago."

I scanned the water carefully. Marovo Lagoon was a big place. What if Jim was wrong? I heard a splash behind me and froze. We had company.

The splash turned out to be the sound of a man in a dugout, the first person we had spotted since leaving Mbili. He was surprised to see us – and fascinated by our boat. He quickly pulled up beside us and ran his hands over the kayak as if he could not believe it was real. While he inspected our boat, he asked us questions about it. He was astonished to hear that we could fold up the kayak and carry it around in a bag.

"You crack it into pieces and you carry it in a sack? Then you take it out of the sack and put it together again?" he asked.

The man's name was Montgomery and he was heading home to his village after working in his garden on this island. When he learned that we were going to Njapuana Island, he offered to guide us there. Njapuana had the only sand beach in this part of the lagoon. It was one of the places where we had Jim's permission to stay.

After hours of paddling, I was looking forward to resting under the tall, tilting palm trees that lined Njapuana's beach. But as we drew close to shore, a coconut shot

down from a tree and – ka-thunk! – hit the water, splashing us. We walked up the beach – bam! Another coconut smashed the sand near us. I looked at the pit it had just made. Suddenly, lounging under a palm tree didn't seem like such a smart idea.

By the time we'd finally found a safe place to set up camp and said goodbye to Montgomery, I was ready for a swim. I turned toward the water. Then I thought about the sharks.

"Come on," said Dag, grabbing his snorkel. "There are sharks all over. That's the way it is here. Besides, most of them are harmless reef sharks ..."

"I know, I know," I interrupted, picking up my snorkel too. "And we're just going to have to get used to having them around." I followed him into the water.

Dag swam out to where the coral reef

We set up our tent close to the shore – away from the palm trees and their falling coconuts.

A Mudskipper Makes its Move

Mudskippers are a kind of fish. They are generally quite shy and they shelter in mangrove swamps where they feed on fish and insects. I was eager to see a mudskipper up close and one day, when we stopped to eat lunch next to some mangrove trees, I got my chance. I had just opened a tin of tuna, and spilled some of it on the ground by accident. Before I knew it, a mudskipper "walked" over to the flakes and devoured them! As it ate, I studied it. This small fish was the size of my index finger and it had gills and fins, just like a "regular" fish. But this fish had done something that most fish never do – it had used its little fins to climb out of the water. I later learned that mudskippers are known for skipping and strolling on land. While there, they breathe moist air that has collected in their gills.

Sharks have been on Earth for hundreds of millions of years, and over time these fish have evolved into skilled hunters. Their sense of smell is so keen that sharks can pick out the blood of a wounded animal in the ocean, even when the injured creature is over half a mile (almost a kilometer) away. Sharks also have excellent eyesight and can see well in dimly-lit water. And that's not all: a shark has a special "sense", called a lateral line, that runs the length of its body. The shark's lateral line helps it detect the vibrations made by other creatures, such as dolphins, as they move through the water.

ended. Meanwhile, I decided to snorkel closer to shore, where I felt safe. I was just starting to relax when the shark slipped up behind me without a sound. As it swam by, I reminded myself to be calm: panicking and thrashing around would only draw more attention to me. It wasn't easy to stay quiet and relaxed. I couldn't help noticing that the shark was almost as long as I was tall. I kept swimming …

Suddenly, when it was out in front, the shark twisted around to face me. It seemed to stare at me coolly, deliberately. Then it turned away and sped off.

Can you spot the snakes slithering along the branches? Look closely — two are hiding here.

Terrified, I lurched out of the water and scrambled over the beach like a crab. Dag was already there. He looked as if he had raced onto the beach in a hurry too.

"Sharks?" I asked, gasping for air.

"Sharks!" he replied, breathing heavily. "How many for you?"

I held up one finger. "Reef shark. Most likely harmless." I stopped to catch my breath. "But then, when it turned to look at me …" I shuddered. "What about you?"

"Two reef sharks," said Dag. "And a huge hammerhead. When it steamed by, everything got out of the way – even me!"

We headed back to our tent. There were no sharks on land to worry about – just some falling coconuts, malaria-bearing mosquitoes, and snakes in the trees. I eyed some hanging vines suspiciously.

Our island paradise was beautiful, but dangers were everywhere. Leaving one danger behind only meant facing another danger in its place – and there was no telling which one might be worse.

Coral: Plant or Animal?

There are many different kinds of coral and most of them look like underwater bushes or branches. But coral aren't plants – they are small animals that are related to jellyfish. The body of each coral is a hollow tube. One end of the coral's tube sticks to a surface, such as the ocean floor. The other end of the tube contains a mouth with stingers and tentacles that the coral uses to catch tiny sea creatures. Coral often grow together in clusters. Coral reefs are made of the hard skeletons of some kinds of coral. These reefs may look tough and solid, but they can be easily destroyed by pollution.

The Garden Beneath the Waves

A coral reef is like a big underwater garden, filled with bird-like fish and coral that looks like plants. To visit this garden, I wore flippers on my feet, a mask over my eyes, and I breathed through an air tube called a snorkel. One end of the snorkel was attached to my mask and stayed in my mouth. The other end poked out of the water into the air.

I felt nervous as I stepped into the water to go snorkelling. Some of my old fear of the water came back and I wondered what lay ahead. I held Dag's hand tightly and together we swam toward the reef.

Curious fish with yellow stripes flocked around us and gazed into our masks. Black angelfish and blue parrot fish flickered by. Then I noticed the reef.

It was dappled with sunlight and covered with coral. I stared at crusty balls of it, green and purply-red. There was staghorn coral with its long branches and brain coral too, patterned with wavy worms. But the most amazing thing were the parrot fish — they were using their "beaks" to break off bits of coral, which they ate!

I let go of Dag's hand and swam on alone. Some large powder-blue mackerel engulfed me. They seemed to stare at me crossly. I smiled and waved them away.

A huge manta ray soared past me in slow motion, gracefully flapping its "wings". Far below it, a turtle snoozed on the ocean floor. I swam close to some giant clams. Their insides looked as soft as velvet and they were the most beautiful shades of blue, green, and red I'd ever seen. I was glad I had come to this hidden garden.

I couldn't get over how beautiful the coral reef was. There were many different kinds of fish and coral everywhere I looked. Amid all this color, I felt like a pale, boring blob!

This pig's pen, like many of the villagers' leaf huts in Chubikopi, stood on stilts over the water of Marovo Lagoon. Narrow spaces between the floor boards allow cool air to flow up from below.

Chapter 3

Come On In!

As we paddled toward the village of Chubikopi, kids raced down to the rocks, waving and calling out to us. But when we pulled onto shore, they suddenly grew shy and ran off, screaming with fear and delight.

Dag and I smiled at the men who had gathered there and asked to see the chief, or other person in charge, just as Jim from Mbili had told us to do. After a moment, the village schoolteacher, a man named David, stepped up to greet

us. He welcomed us to Chubikopi and invited us to stay with his family.

The men crowded around the kayak while we tied it to the stilts of a leaf hut. One man climbed into it, while others studied the kayak and our paddles. Some of the kids drifted back and squeezed in between the adults for a closer look too.

While Dag answered all the men's questions, girls grabbed me by the hand and led me along a narrow path made of coconut husks to a leaf hut. I felt cool,

Where Am I Now?

We saw a place in Chubikopi where war canoe replicas are still made. The old name for them is "Tomoko".

Marovo Lagoon

Chubikopi

Njapuana Island

I helped prepare a Solomons meal here — it was delicious. My favorite dish was slippery cabbage cooked with coconut and canned tuna.

As we kayaked here, sunlight bounced off the water and the white sand beaches, dazzling my eyes. It was hot and muggy, too — I felt like I was being roasted, boiled, and fried, all at once.

Almost every bit of land in the Solomons, no matter how small it is, belongs to someone. I wondered who owned this tiny island ...

Building a War Canoe

It takes several years, the parts of five different kinds of trees, lots of planning, and careful work to build a war canoe (see small photo). In ancient times, these boats carried raiding warriors to the villages of their enemies. The very first thing that the unlucky villagers would have seen was the figurehead on the boat's prow (see main photo).

refreshing air on my feet as I walked over a floor made of split bamboo cane. The walls and roof of the leaf hut were made entirely of plants from the jungle – there were no bricks, nails, or concrete anywhere. I glanced through the floor slats. It was about six feet (two meters) to the water below and, judging by all the women and children around me, the floor was holding up a lot of weight. I hoped that everything was as sturdy as it looked.

After Dag joined me, David showed us around the village. We saw the store, the

school, and a place where a war canoe was being made. Then it was time to prepare dinner. I joined David's wife, Merver, in a smoky cooking hut to help out.

"When I saw you in your canoe," she told me, "I couldn't stop laughing. You looked very funny! It is custom for us to paddle – not you!"

I told her about Dag's dream of learning how to kayak and how he had taught the two of us to become paddlers. Merver wanted to know more about Dag and me. "Did your mother and father choose him

Schools in the Jungle

If you attended a school in the Solomon Islands, you might sit in a classroom like this, with floors of coral stone or dirt and open windows that look out onto the jungle. Your lessons would be taught in three languages – English, Pidgin, as well as the language spoken in your part of the Solomons.

Taro root looks like this before it's roasted.

to be your husband?" she asked.

I explained that, where Dag and I came from, men and women usually picked their own mates. If an unmarried man and woman found that they were well-suited and loved each other, then they might decide to get married.

"Really!" replied Merver. "It's not always that way here. When I was nineteen, my parents chose David for me – I was cross! They said he was a good man and would care for me. He had to pay a big bride price for me."

Merver motioned to a heap of cassava roots on a table next to us. "David had to give many cassava, like these. And floor mats and a pig, too."

While we talked, Merver roasted some taro and cassava roots on hot stones heated

Bathrooms in the Jungle

Some of the village bathrooms I used were on stilts, out in the lagoon. To reach them, I had to stroll along walkways that stretched above the water (see main photo). Inside, I might find toilet paper made from a stringy coconut husk (see small photo). And when I peeked out between the bathroom wall boards, I always had a spectacular view!

in a fire pit. Then she showed me how to prepare slippery cabbage for our meal. This green vegetable looked a bit like spinach. I separated the stems from the long, narrow leaves and shredded the leaves.

Merver squeezed thick, white juice from some freshly-grated coconut and put the juice in a pot with some water. She added the slippery cabbage and a can of tuna I had given her. Then she simmered the mixture over the fire until the taro and cassava roots were ready. As we carried the food up to the house, its delicious smell wafted all around us.

When the sun set, David lit kerosene lamps, filling the house with soft light. To my surprise, I could hear a faint, familiar sound in the distance. It was Madonna singing on someone's radio! Her voice and the sounds of fruit bats squabbling in the trees were the last things I heard before I fell asleep on my floor mat, out on David and Merver's porch.

Before dawn, an archer fish swimming under the porch squirted me. It was trying to "shoot" an insect with a mouthful of water. Instead, it had hit me. I peered through the floor slats to the water below. I couldn't find the archer fish, but I did see our kayak, still tied to the house stilts.

Soon Dag and I would be back inside our kayak, paddling towards Roviana Lagoon. I glanced at the shores of the nearby islands and the mangrove trees that grew there. I had heard that crocodiles still lived in Roviana Lagoon. Would we run into some or were crocodiles a rare sight? I would know the answer soon.

A dugout canoe is made from a solid tree trunk that is slowly hollowed out and shaped with hand tools (see small photo, above). Our kayak wasn't made of wood: it had a "skin" of waterproof material stretched over an aluminum and plastic frame. All dugouts are open from the front to the back. Our kayak, on the other hand, contained two separate cockpits, the places where Dag and I sat. Our kayak could hold a maximum of two passengers – big dugouts can hold many people at once!

What are Some of the Differences Between Dugouts and Kayaks?

In Nusa Hope (see below), I discovered just how fast a crocodile could move. One moment this one seemed to be resting – and the next moment it was lunging at me!

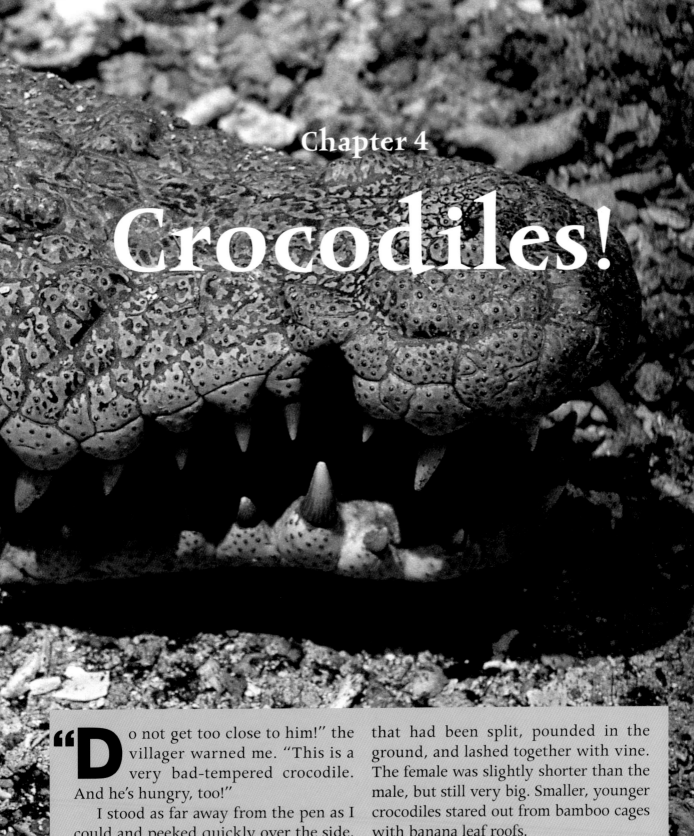

Chapter 4
Crocodiles!

"**D**o not get too close to him!" the villager warned me. "This is a very bad-tempered crocodile. And he's hungry, too!"

I stood as far away from the pen as I could and peeked quickly over the side. There he was: a saltwater crocodile, the length of a tall man. A female crocodile was in a separate pen, also made of logs that had been split, pounded in the ground, and lashed together with vine. The female was slightly shorter than the male, but still very big. Smaller, younger crocodiles stared out from bamboo cages with banana leaf roofs.

It seemed so strange that I, who feared crocodiles, was here by these pens on Nusa Hope Island. Earlier in the day,

The school in this village was pretty big – it had six classrooms. Only one room had desks for the kids to sit at. I sat there and gazed out the window at palm trees and hibiscus bushes with big, red blooms.

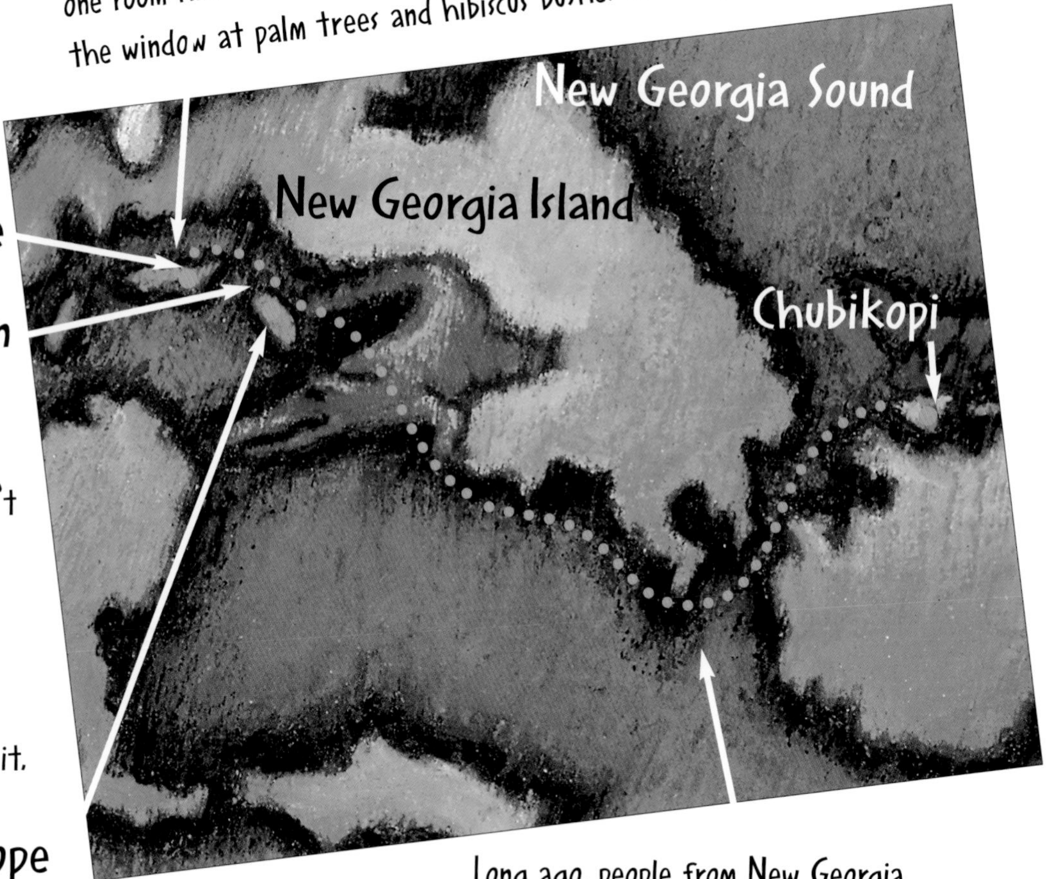

New Georgia Sound

New Georgia Island

Chubikopi

Baraula Village

Roviana Lagoon

The water in this lagoon was so shallow that big boats couldn't go here. We had to watch out for sharp coral that could slice open the bottom of our kayak, damaging it.

Nusa Hope

After my close encounter with a crocodile here, I didn't want to see another one of these reptiles ever again. There was only one problem: a villager said Roviana Lagoon was swimming with them!

Long ago, people from New Georgia Island were head-hunters. They travelled to other islands, killed the men who lived there, and returned with the heads of their victims.

Wild Wild Crocodiles

The only way to look at a crocodile this close is when it's inside a pen with sturdy walls. I didn't want to think about what it would be like to see the same sight out in the wild – an unprotected person wouldn't have a chance against this big, tough-skinned predator.

we'd met a fisherman and asked him if there were crocodiles in Roviana Lagoon. He had assumed that Dag and I wanted to see some and so he had invited us to come to Nusa Hope. I hadn't wanted to go, but neither Dag nor I felt it would be polite to refuse his invitation. So here we were, face-to-face with some saltwater crocodiles. The only thing standing between us and them were some logs and vines.

Yet I wasn't as terrified as I would have been several days ago. After visiting the houses in Chubikopi, I knew that buildings made of jungle plants were sturdier than they looked. The dwellings in Chubikopi were flexible enough and strong enough to

support the weight of entire families. These pens had to be tough enough to hold the crocodiles, I figured.

I looked into the female's pen again. She was sound asleep. She looked the same way I felt: hot and too tired to move. Although there was nothing ferocious about her, I was still glad that she was penned in.

"You must be careful!" the villager repeated. This time his voice was sharp.

As he spoke, the female's stubby legs seemed to swell and stretch. She rose and lunged at me, slamming the logs and snapping her jaws. I jumped back. The logs shook … Only a moment ago they had seemed strong. Now, I wasn't sure.

The house we stayed at in Baraula was under construction, so we set up our tent there and slept in it. The tent protected us from the mosquitoes that spread malaria disease.

When we arrived in a village, our kayak would disappear for ages: the chief was trying it out. Gideon liked kayaking too.

Another villager spoke. "The female thinks you will take her eggs." He pointed inside the pen to a pile of dirt where they lay.

"Not me!" I babbled in a shaky voice. My heart pounded in my ears. "Not me – I wouldn't dream of it!"

Much later, after I had calmed down, I asked the men where the crocodiles had come from, hoping that it wasn't near by. They looked at me as if they couldn't believe I was asking such a silly question.

"From the water here," one of them said to me, pointing toward Roviana Lagoon. He nodded at some mangroves in the direction we would soon be heading. "And from the shore, there."

First it had been sharks in the water – now it was crocodiles. I didn't like the idea of having either one around, but then I didn't have much choice …

By the time we reached the village of Baraula, the memory of my frightening encounter had faded a little. Gideon, the senior elder in Baraula, invited us to stay there in a house that was still under construction. Beneath its open rafters, where shark fins had been hung to dry, we set up our tent. Kids sat by the house, silently watching Dag and me as if we were actors performing a play in a theater.

"The children are not always like this," Gideon said when he came by later. "It is just that many of them have never seen white people before."

As night fell, I watched a villager blow into a conch shell, making a loud trumpeting sound. "It is time for everyone to go home to bed," Gideon told us. The kids vanished and Dag and I settled down to sleep with only each other for company.

In Baraula, we met a man with an opossum that he had saved after its mother died. This baby looked tame but when I held it, it bit me!

During the night, I awoke and headed for the "bathroom" that I had used earlier, out by the lagoon. As I shone my flashlight over the big banana leaves that lay along the path, I tried not to think about the crocodiles that might be lurking by the shore. But that was impossible: all I could think about were crocodiles and their huge jaws and powerful bodies.

It was no use telling myself that the women of Baraula walked along this path and others close by it to get to the same bathroom I was heading to. Sure, it was probably safe here most of the time – but what if tonight a crocodile happened to be here right when I was? Each year, I knew, there were reports of people in villages being carried off and eaten by crocodiles. Crocodile attacks didn't happen often but when they did, they were deadly.

I was so caught up in worrying about crocodiles that I almost stepped directly on a centipede that lay in the path. But this was no ordinary centipede. It was nearly as long as my foot and very scary. If I had stepped on it, it would have given me a painful bite that caused a fever.

The thought of that, along with the crocodiles, was almost enough to make me turn back. But I kept going. Today had been a day of close calls with dangerous creatures. All I could hope was that our good luck wouldn't run out.

Times are Changing ...

In the past, people in the Solomons made a living by fishing, growing food in gardens, and collecting materials from the jungle to build dugouts and houses. Money wasn't usually needed to buy things. Today, things are different. Many people want to own outboard motors for their boats, and radios and cassette players are also becoming popular. To buy these things, people need money. Families also need money to pay for their children's secondary education. It's not easy for people to make lots of money in a village and so many villagers (especially young people) move to the larger towns with the hope of finding paying work. While there, they encounter many modern ways of life that are very different from the traditional ways they have known.

Gigantic Creatures

From giant centipedes to giant clams, there are lots of enormous creatures to be found in the Solomons. Many of these creatures are dangerous, too. A giant clam (see right) has a powerful grip and it can trap your hand if you stick it in the clam's open jaws.

Inside this wooden "house" are the skulls of ancient chiefs. The house holds much wealth too — that's shell money, a kind of traditional currency, underneath the skulls.

Chapter 5
Land of the Skulls

The skulls gazed at me empty-eyed while I stared back. There were dozens of them. Some were covered with creeping green moss. Others had plant roots running through them like tough, tangled veins. Around the skulls lay human arm bones, leg bones, and a chipped clay pipe.

Where Am I Now?

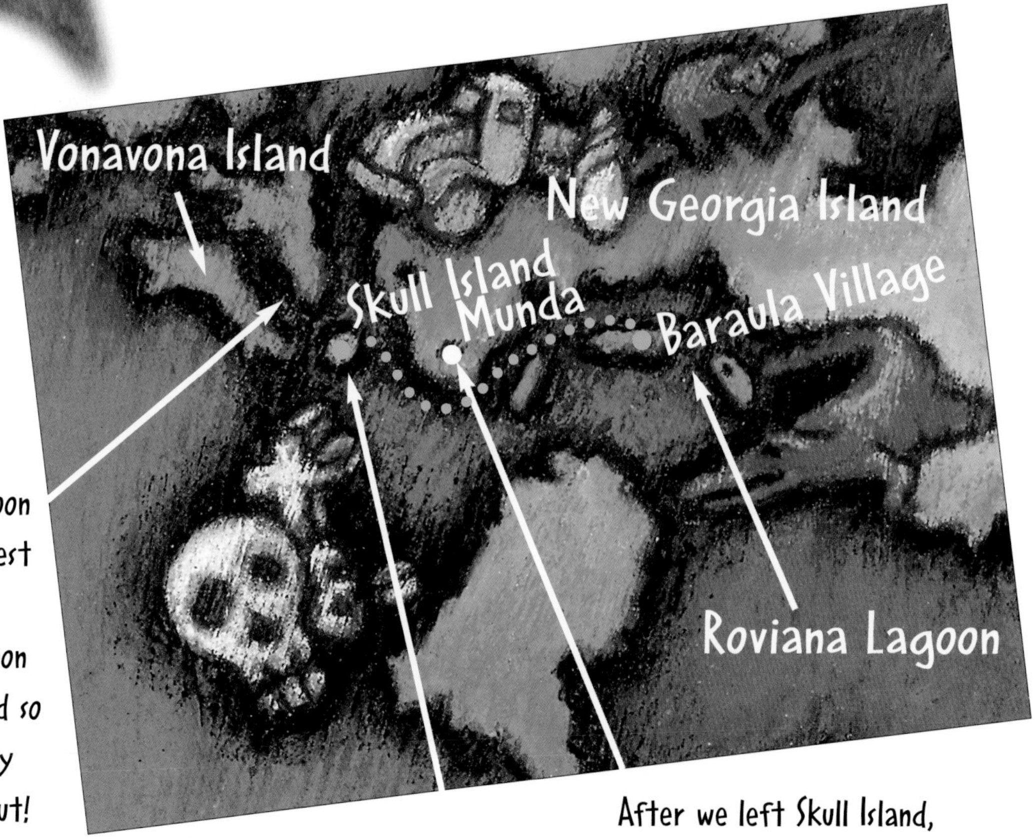

Vonavona Island

New Georgia Island

Skull Island
Munda

Baraula Village

Roviana Lagoon

Vonavona Lagoon was the smallest and the most beautiful lagoon we had visited so far — it really knocked me out! I saw blue-spotted stingrays and small purple jellyfish in the shallow water.

The heads of dead chiefs were kept here, along with heads gathered during head-hunting expeditions. Before we could visit Skull Island, we had to get permission from the person who owns this place.

After we left Skull Island, we paddled here and boarded a ferry back to Honiara. Soon we would be on our way to Santa Isabel Island, the place where many of the skulls had come from.

Almost everywhere I looked, I saw skulls. The ones in these rocks seemed to peek out at us.

We were standing by a tall pile of rocks on Skull Island, in Vonavona Lagoon. Skull Island was the place where the heads of dead chiefs and other people were kept. Coming here hadn't been easy. First we had to find the chief of the local area and get his permission to visit the island. The chief arranged for his eldest son, Pitu, to accompany us. According to Pitu, there was an important reason why he had to go with Dag and me.

"Skull Island is a 'tambu' place," he told us. "It is forbidden for outsiders to come here alone. If you did, you would be struck down with sickness. And perhaps you would even die."

Carefully, I stepped around a skull on the ground and took a better look at the

Modern-day chiefs are buried here, in graves.

What is Shell Money?

Long ago, pieces of certain sea shells were used as currency in the Solomons. Today, some shell money is still used as "bride price", the payment that an unmarried man makes to the family of his bride-to-be before the couple marries. Sometimes people wear shell money around their neck, like jewellery. The shell money on Skull Island (see left) is made from the shells of giant clams. Other shell money is made from pearl and oyster shells.

carved chest on top of the rock-pile. The chest, Pitu told us, was made of a kind of wood that could withstand rot and decay. Inside it were layers of skulls, surrounded by some shell money made from giant clam shells. Long ago, clam shell money had been the traditional currency in this part of the Solomon Islands.

"Before white people came, we put our chiefs' heads in here," said Pitu, nodding to the chest. "This is the place where my great-grandfather is. Other heads, much older, are here too."

He pointed to a gravestone with a cross on it. "After the missionaries arrived, the chiefs were given Christian burials. My grandfather is buried under that stone."

"And the other skulls – what about them?" I asked him, pointing to the ones tucked in the rocks and lying on the ground around our feet.

"Many are from Santa Isabel Island," Pitu replied. "Our people took the men's heads and brought back fair-haired women as slaves. In the times before, our people believed that a man's head held all his life force, all his power. That is why the people here once hunted heads on Santa Isabel."

I listened carefully as Pitu spoke of Santa Isabel. Soon, we would be going there. To get to that island, we would kayak to a place called Munda and board a ferry to Honiara, the capital city. From Honiara, we would catch another boat that would take us to Santa Isabel. It was the longest island in the Solomons and there

Water Tanks and World War II

The Solomon Islands, and the sea around them, were the site of fierce air, land, and sea battles between the Japanese and Allied forces during World War II. Although this war ended more than 50 years ago, you can still spot reminders of it: there are abandoned army vehicles on land and crashed planes underwater. You can also see wartime objects that have been put to new uses. The skinny tank (right) was once part of a plane and held fuel. Today, the tank holds water.

would be much to explore there.

"Santa Isabel Island! That's where we are going," I told Pitu.

I wasn't sure what to make of his answer. "There are not many people on that island anymore," he said, looking at me and shaking his head.

As we walked away from the skulls, I wondered what was waiting for us on Santa Isabel. We had heard that giant turtles and monitor lizards lived there, but what else would we find? In a few days time we would see for ourselves — and I could hardly wait.

A lagoon is a body of water separated from the sea by a coral reef. Vonavona Lagoon, where tiny Skull Island sat, was the loveliest lagoon we had seen so far.

What about Women?

In the towns, women work side by side with men in banks and offices. In the villages, women also do a lot of the same work as men — they paddle dugouts, they work in gardens, they help build houses — and they are very strong physically. But women do not always have the same freedoms as men, especially in the most remote parts of the Solomons.

In those places, there are still lots of traditional "rules" that a woman must obey in her daily life. For instance, a woman can only use the paddle with the circle-shaped end, shown below. She is forbidden from using the paddle next to it — that's a man's paddle and only men can use it.

However, traditions to do with women are changing in the Solomons. At one time, a woman's husband was chosen by her parents or other relatives. These days, women are more likely to choose their own husbands. And today, women tend to receive more education than they did in the past.

Women who live in the villages do a lot of the same things as men — they work in the gardens, they help build houses, and they paddle dugouts.

Even at a little market like Honiara's (see main photo), it took time to pick out what we needed. All markets sell green and orange betel nuts (see above and right). People like to chew the ripe kernel of the betel nut.

Chapter 6
Into the Unknown

As I walked down the main street of Honiara, I looked at a traffic light and recalled a story that someone had told me. A few years earlier, when this traffic light had first gone up, it had immediately caused a traffic jam — everyone with a vehicle had driven to the light to try it out. Today, it was still the only traffic light in this crowded town surrounded by jungle.

Honiara was dusty and small. It didn't have modern stores or many restaurants. But Honiara was a big, bustling place compared to the remote areas where we were going. We weren't sure what we would find on Santa Isabel, so we bought all the

Where Am I Now?

We were in a wild, lonely place and I suddenly remembered that we'd left our two-way radio back in Honiara. There was no point bringing it with us, we figured — there wouldn't be many people around to rescue us if we ran into trouble.

Santa Isabel Island

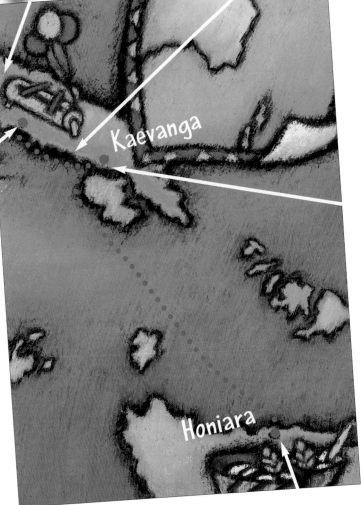

Kaevanga

Kilokaka

What a happy, noisy place this was! Loud drumming from the church next door woke us in the morning. Kids followed us wherever we went, playing with the balloons we gave them.

A lifeboat from the cargo boat dropped us off here. We assembled our kayak and paddled away. Were we heading into a great adventure? Or were we putting ourselves in grave danger? There was only one way to find out . . .

Honiara

We returned to Honiara, where we stocked up at the market, then boarded a cargo boat to Santa Isabel. Before we left, I spotted a crab crossing the road. Some cars almost hit it, but the crab just shook a claw at them and kept going.

Going to the Market

At an open-air market, you can buy peanuts, green peppers, or parrot fish (above left). The goods you purchase often come in bags woven from plant leaves (above right).

supplies we could in Honiara. We stocked up on milk powder, sugar, tea, rice, and cans of tuna from the small shops. At the open-air market, we purchased some sweet potatoes and long, thick coils of tobacco that we could trade later on for vegetables, fruit, and other supplies.

The first time we'd come to this market, before taking the ferry to Minjanga Island, everything had seemed unusual. I'd been surprised to find that there were almost no plastic bags or containers anywhere at the market. This time, I knew what to expect. The items that we purchased were given to us in shopping bags made from banana and palm leaves. These shopping bags, I thought, were much more attractive than modern ones made of plastic and they were just as useful, too.

As we left the market, my thoughts

Baby Time

In the village of Kilokaka, we saw this friendly baby fruit bat. Dag liked it so much that he wanted to take the bat with us — he thought it could travel in our kayak and be our boat's mascot! But in the end we both decided it would be best to leave the bat where we found it, here with the people of Kilokaka.

We saw many frigate birds near Santa Isabel. Their babies look like fluffy balls of feathers.

turned from shopping bags to Santa Isabel. I tried to imagine what lay ahead on our journey. According to our maps, the coastline of Santa Isabel Island was very exposed. There wasn't much of an outlying reef to protect our kayak from large waves. And there were other things to consider. What if one of us got sick or was attacked by a shark? Pitu had told us that there were few people on the island. How would we reach someone to help us — and what kind of aid could we expect to find in such an isolated place? Were we heading into a great adventure, one that we wouldn't want to miss? Or were we putting ourselves in grave danger?

Much later, as we kayaked towards the village of Kilokaka on Santa Isabel Island, I still didn't have the answers to any of my questions. All I could see was a rocky island coast with steep hills at the top and thick jungle that reached almost to the water's edge in some places. In the sky,

Giving and Receiving

People in the Solomons, like most people in the world, have strong beliefs to do with giving and receiving. They believe that a person who receives food, goods, or lodging owes a debt to the giver and must repay the giver with things of equal value. That's why Dag and I carried a supply of fish hooks, tobacco, balloons, and other items with us wherever we went. Sometimes we left them as gifts in the villages we visited. Other times, we traded our things for food.

frigate birds circled together, making huge "cyclones" as they flapped up and away from us. Strong waves pounded the shore. It seemed that we were the only people in this wild, lonely place.

Then, at last, we came to Kilokaka. Villagers stood on the beach, watching us paddle in. The sight of them made me grin. We weren't so alone after all!

As the bow of our kayak nudged the shore, an old man presented us with two green coconuts. Dag and I stepped out of our kayak and grabbed some of our bags. We were about to unpack the rest when lots of helpful villagers lifted the kayak out of the water and placed it on the shore. They carried away our bags while Dag and I trailed slowly behind them.

We found our bags piled just outside an empty leaf hut. The village organizer, a man named James, stood by them. "We were expecting you," he told us.

It's time to rise! Can we come in and visit?

His words surprised me. We had seen only a handful of people since arriving at Santa Isabel, yet somehow word of our presence had reached Kilokaka before we showed up. James spoke to us again. "Your house is ready. Please come in."

As he led us inside, James explained that every village on Santa Isabel has a leaf hut that is always kept empty. This leaf hut, called a rest house, is for any special visitors who come to the village. "You are the first white visitors we have had here in three years," he said.

I quickly realized that the last thing we would have to worry about was being on our own. Many villagers crowded into our hut, especially after they heard that we wanted to trade some of our things for fresh fruit. We traded balloons, fishing hooks, and the tobacco from the Honiara market for some pineapples, bananas, and oranges. Soon we had more fruit than we needed and we had almost run out of the balloons. None of the children had ever seen them and everyone wanted one!

After dark, the women and children

Long, loud thumps from the slit drum next door to our tent beat us awake before dawn.

And the Beat Goes On ...

Some ancient Solomons traditions are still passed from one generation to the next. These boys are performing a dance that their elders taught them. It was once used to celebrate big events like the end of a war. When the boys grow up, they'll be able to keep this tradition alive by teaching the dance to their kids.

returned to their homes but the men stayed until well past midnight. They wanted to know all about our way of life back home. "How many people are in your village?" they asked us. "Does everyone there have a boat like yours?" Finally, they left and we fell asleep.

But not for long. Before dawn, long, loud drumming from the church hut next door beat us awake. I opened my eyes. "Still worried that there won't be enough people around on Santa Isabel? That we

might get lonely?" Dag asked with a yawn.

I looked out the window. A crowd of kids had already gathered there. Each one of them stared at me hopefully, silently waiting to be invited in.

"Oh, all right," I said to them, smiling. I patted the floor next to me. "Come on in!"

I could sleep another time. Right now, it was more important to be with these kids. They wanted to know all about me – and I was eager to find out about their life on Santa Isabel Island, too.

A House Made of Plants

Traditional houses in the Solomons are made entirely from vines, leaves and other plant and tree parts gathered from the jungle, then tied or sewn together by hand (see small photo): there are no nails, bricks, or concrete anywhere. Buildings made of plants may look flimsy, but they are very sturdy.

All night, strange creatures rose out of the surf, came ashore, then plunged back into the misty waves.

I'd never seen anything like this huge creature before. It had a wide, leathery back and was about as long as a bathtub.

Chapter 7

Make Way for Giants

The deep marks on the beach were fresh. Even in the dark, I could see they were huge: they looked like they had been made by the caterpillar tracks of a bull-dozer. But that was impossible. There were no roads on this part of Santa Isabel Island, no way at all for vehicles to get here.

The tracks led from the sea and up the beach, to some bushes. As Dag and I crept toward the bushes, we heard deep, breathy grunts. With each grunt, I grew more curious and nervous. What were we about to find on this deserted beach?

The sounds grew louder as we crept closer. Dag snapped on his

Where Am I Now?

Before we left Kilokaka, James told us about the giant leatherbacks and the place, farther up the coast, where they came ashore this time of year. He said that, if we were lucky, we might see them.

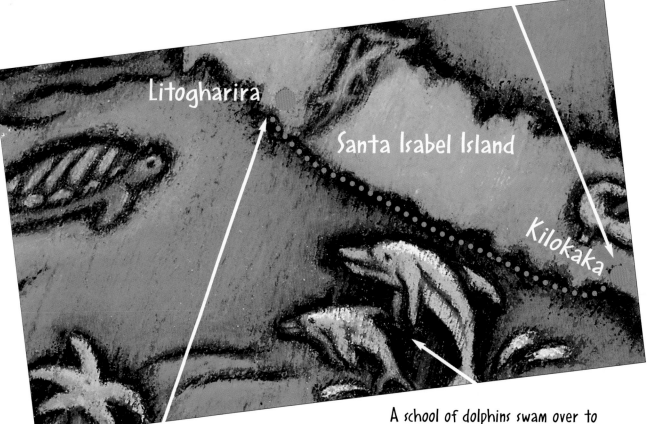

Litogharira

Santa Isabel Island

Kilokaka

Once a year, giant turtles swim here to lay their eggs on land. Dag and I watched them come and go throughout the night. We weren't the only ones around — some egg-eating lizards also dropped by.

A school of dolphins swam over to our kayak. They were all around us, feeding and playing, leaping out of the water and twirling around. Sunlight glinted off their sleek grey bodies and shiny pale bellies.

Only a bulldozer could make these tracks. That's what I thought – before I spotted the turtles.

flashlight – and that's when we saw the leatherback turtle. From front to back it was as long as a bathtub. The top of its ridged shell reached up to my thighs.

Both Dag and I had wanted to see the leatherback turtles ever since we heard that they came to this particular beach to lay their eggs. This only happened once a year and we felt very fortunate to be here at just the right time.

The turtle was so busy scooping up sand with her flippers that she didn't notice us. After she dug a deep, narrow nest hole, she began laying eggs, four at a time. They were the size of small chicken eggs and looked soft, not big and hard as I had expected. As the eggs fell from her body, jelly-like tears flowed from the turtle's eyes.

In just one night, a female leatherback must dig a nest hole and lay a hundred eggs in it.

Turtle alert! An egg-eating lizard has arrived.

Laying eggs looked like very hard work.

The turtle rested after she filled her nest with many eggs – dozens of them. Then she covered them with sand and filled in the hole. Her movements were gentle as if she somehow knew that one wrong move might crack all her eggs.

I thought she was finished, but instead she hauled herself along the beach. She dug another hole there and filled it in. There were no eggs in this nest and that puzzled me until I remembered something James from Kilokaka had told me.

I nudged Dag. He was staring at the very same place with a questioning look. "That's a decoy nest hole," I whispered. "So the lizards will search for eggs there, instead of eating the ones in the first hole."

Meanwhile, the mother turtle returned to the sea. Other turtles rose out of the surf and trudged up the beach. As one left us at dawn, Dag prepared to take a photo of it. He set up his camera on a tripod, well out of the way of the turtle. He was about to shoot when the turtle changed direction

A monitor lizard roams the beach. It waits for the leatherbacks to leave, then devours their eggs for breakfast.

and headed straight toward him. There was no stopping her – she was powerful enough to mow down anything in her path. "Get out of the way," I yelled.

Dag did, but just in the nick of time. "So much for that shot," he said ruefully, picking himself up off the ground.

"Never mind," I said. "Look at this." Monitor lizards were digging up the eggs

and devouring them. The eggs were just hours old and already they were gone. They hadn't had much chance to survive.

But then there were the huge, full-grown turtles we had seen ... They had started out as eggs and somehow they had survived lizards and other dangers. Perhaps some of the turtles in these eggs would make it too. And one night, years from now, some of them would come here to lay their eggs and begin the cycle once again.

The last turtle was plodding out to sea. As I walked beside her, I touched her shell. It felt leathery, just as I thought it would. Dag joined me and we each gave her one last pat on the back.

"Goodbye!" we called out as the waves spilled over her shell. "Goodbye!"

One day, off Kora Island, we swam
around the wreck of an old fighter plane.
Decades ago, during World War II, this plane
had been in air battles and fired its guns
over the Solomons. After being shot down,
it had crashed in the water. Now fish
roamed its cockpit and coral coated its wings.

Chapter 8

Diving into Adventure

"**D**o not go! We will build a house for you!" our host called out.

We thanked Victor for his generous offer. From the moment he had spotted Dag and me paddling near Kora Island, Victor had made us feel warmly welcome here. He and his family, who lived some of the time in Honiara and some of the time on Kora, owned few belongings but they shared everything they had with us.

Each day on Kora unfolded the same way. At dawn, Christina, Victor's wife, slid a jar of freshly-picked orchids under the mosquito netting that hung over us while we slept. After a slow, lazy start to the day, we went fishing with the women

Where Am I Now?

We explored the wreck of an old fighter plane that had crashed in the water. It was calm and peaceful here, just as it was everywhere around Kora.

We got lost about here.

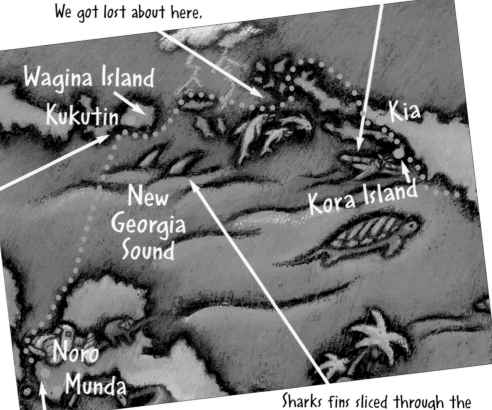

Wagina Island
Kukutin

Kia

New Georgia Sound

Kora Island

Noro
Munda

Bad news here — the ship we planned to board had already left. We had no choice but to keep paddling.

More bad news here — the ferry we planned to take to Honiara had left early. If only we could get to Munda — we heard that there were planes there that could take us to Honiara . . .

Sharks fins sliced through the waves. But I didn't care — I was so hot I had to go for a swim. I waited until the fins left, then plunged into the sea.

This shot of Dag, me, and Victor's family always makes me grin. We had great times on Kora.

and listened to them sing as they paddled their dugout. Before dinner, we helped gather firewood in the mangrove swamps. After dark we sat outside, under a canopy of stars. Sometimes we talked with Victor and his family. Other times we sat silently, listening to the waves lap the shore. I felt happy and peaceful here.

"Do you realize," said Dag one night, "we have less than a month left before it's time to leave the Solomons? And we can't stay here longer than that – we have to fly out on the date that's on our plane tickets."

Reluctantly, I considered Dag's words. I had lost track of time – and there was still so much that we had to do before we left the Solomons. We wanted to explore the northern part of Santa Isabel Island. Then we planned to cross the Manning Strait to Wagina Island and take a ferry back to Honiara. To do those things we had to leave Kora Island as soon as possible.

After we sadly said goodbye to Victor and his family, we stopped at Kia, a large village up the coast, to replenish our food and other supplies. Then we headed for the Manning Strait. Getting there turned out to be more difficult than we expected.

Along the way we got lost in some tiny islands that weren't correctly charted on our map. Then we ran dangerously low on water before finding more in a stream on land. And always, there was the fear that danger of some kind – sharks, sickness, bad weather – lay ahead. There was no one around to help us if we ran into trouble.

Finally, we found the Manning Strait. Powerful currents and high winds were churning it into steep waves. We paddled for hours and we were exhausted when we reached Kukutin, on Wagina Island. Here we planned to board a ferry to Honiara.

Leafy, Breezy, Shady Ways

These girls have found an all-natural way to beat the heat – they're using huge leaves to shade themselves from the fierce sun. Smaller leaves are handy too. You can grasp them by the stem and wave them like a fan to make an instant breeze.

There was only one problem: the last ferry before Christmas had sailed earlier that day. After so much effort, we had missed it! The next ferry would arrive too late for us to catch our flight. How would we make it back to Honiara in time?

"We'll have to paddle to Noro," I said. Noro was a port on New Georgia Island and another ship bound for Honiara was scheduled to leave from there in two days.

It was a long paddle to Noro and we would be in open ocean for an entire day. Up until now, we had mostly been kayaking in coastal waters where the reefs protected us from large ocean waves. Kayaking to Noro would be extremely difficult to do, even under the best conditions.

I did not want to think about what would happen to us on the open ocean if there were storms, high winds, or rough

Compared to Kora, the village of Kia seemed huge. It had a big church adorned with shells.

waves. And even with calm wind and water, there was still the heat and humidity to deal with. But we had no choice: it was the only way we could reach Honiara in time to board our plane.

At dawn, as we left for Noro, there was no wind at all, not even a breeze to help cool us. By mid-morning, a thick, smothering blanket of heat was wrapped around us. Although we had slathered ourselves in sunscreen, our sweat washed it away and the sun burned deep into our skin. Soon I noticed almost nothing but the heat and bright glare. My hands were so sweaty I could hardly grip the paddle. The horizon danced before my eyes.

The ocean seemed as thick as syrup and it was all I could do to push my paddle through it, again … and again. Every muscle in my arms screamed out in pain. My legs grew numb. The hours crawled by.

Shortly before midnight, we dropped an anchor to keep the kayak from drifting. Then we scrunched down in our seats and fell asleep, exhausted. Several hours later, we awoke tired and damp. We pushed our paddles through the water and glided on

Our drinking water was nearly gone when we stopped to rest and eat on this island. Luckily, we found a freshwater stream near the trees.

The longest, hardest day of my life began when we left Wagina Island to paddle to Noro.

The heat seemed to eat me alive. I stripped off my shirt, then the sun scorched my skin.

into the dark. I was beyond caring if we made it to Noro. My arms seemed to move on their own, over and over …

Finally, thirty hours after we had set out from Kukutin, we saw the buoy marking the harbor of Noro. The longest day of my life had finally come to an end.

I was so weak that I could hardly stand on the busy, crowded wharf and I couldn't get used to the noise and activity that swirled around us. A policeman named Edwin came over to see if we needed help. We explained that we had come here to catch the ferry to Honiara. Edwin looked apologetic. Then he told us something that I could hardly believe.

The last ferry to Honiara had left early. Edwin couldn't explain why it had left, just that it was gone. The next ferry to Honiara would arrive in Noro early in the New Year, too late for us.

Once again, we had missed the boat. I turned to Dag. He looked as exhausted and discouraged as I felt. When I opened my mouth, all that came out was a dry, raspy croak. "There has to be a way back to Honiara. There has to be!"

I gazed out the window as our bush plane sprang off the runway and buzzed toward the clouds. All I could think was, "We did it – we finally found a way back to Honiara!"

Chapter 9

Up, Up, and Away

I nudged Dag in the seat next to me. "Look, there's Skull Island!" We crowded against one of the little windows in the plane for a last look. Then Skull Island slipped out of view and we leaned back in our seats.

It seemed incredible that we were here, in a bush plane, finally on our way to Honiara. And it was all thanks to Edwin, the policeman in Noro. He told us that there was a new road that ran through the jungle and connected Noro to the town of Munda. At Munda, he said, there was an airstrip and bush planes that regularly flew to Honiara. Edwin telephoned Munda, booked a

Where Am I Now?

Munda

Honiara

N
W ✛ E
S

We had covered a lot of ground — and water — during our time in the Solomons. That's what I realized as we flew from Munda to Honiara and I looked down at some of the places we'd been to ...

As the plane swung low over Vangunu Island, I took one last look at the village of Chubikopi.

flight for us, and arranged for a truck to take us to the airstrip. Almost before we had time to thank him, Dag and I were on our way to Munda to catch this plane.

I leaned over to Dag and looked down at the turquoise water of Roviana Lagoon. "That must be Baraula Village," I said, pointing to a cluster of houses by the shore. "I can still picture Gideon in our kayak – he really looked at home in it!"

That reminded me of something else we had seen there. "Do you remember the boy who was 'kayaking' in his little dugout, close to the shore?" I asked Dag.

"Sure I do," Dag replied with a grin. "I couldn't get over the kind of paddle he had!" The little boy from Baraula had been using something we'd never seen before in

the Solomons: a kayak-style paddle with a blade on either end, instead of a "regular" dugout paddle with only one blade.

"Someone must have carved it for him after noticing our paddles," I said. "Like it or not, I guess we've introduced something new to the Solomons."

Minutes later, our plane flew over Marovo Lagoon. "Look out for Dracula," I joked. I half-expected to see him, circling over the water with his large, dark wings as he kept an eye out for intruders. But there was no sign of him anywhere.

Dag pointed down at the reef showing through the water. "That's the place where I saw that huge hammerhead, right after you ran into the reef shark."

Our close encounters with those sharks

seemed long ago. And now I wasn't so afraid of sharks – they had become part of our daily life. We had seen so many strange sights during our trip … the leatherback turtles laying their eggs in the night … the giant centipede I almost stepped on … the crocodiles at Nusa Hope … and all those skulls on Skull Island. I'd had so many fears about our trip and so few ideas of what to expect. Perhaps that's what had made it such an amazing adventure.

I realized how accustomed I'd grown to looking out at the jungle from our kayak, eating fresh coconut meat with a little spoon made of coconut shell, and snorkelling over coral reefs while parrot fish swam beside me. I would miss many things that I could only find here, from the kids who showed us how to chew sugar cane to the beautiful views I saw from the open-air bathrooms that stood over the ocean.

I thought again of our stay with Victor and his family on the island of Kora and the freshly-picked orchids that they had placed next to us each morning. Then, with a smile, I recalled Victor's last words to us as we left Kora. He and his family had climbed into their dugout to accompany us as far as the outer reef. As they paddled, they sang a beautiful song of farewell. I could still hear them singing after we crossed the reef and their dugout disappeared from view.

Then – suddenly – a new sound. It was Victor, calling out to us one last time.

"Maria, Dag! Do not forget your time on our island – we will be here, waiting for you!"

INDEX

FURTHER RESOURCES: WEBSITES

Solomon Islands Index Page at: http://www.tcol.co.uk/solomon/solomon.htm
Want to see what the Solomon Islands flag looks like or learn the words to its national anthem? Then drop into this fact-filled website: adults and kids can gather basic information about the Solomons here.

Fieldwork Photo Gallery - Solomon Islands, 1998 at:
http://www.austmus.gov.au/science/division/vert/ichth/fieldwork/solomons/
When researchers from museums in Australia and the U.S. travelled to the Solomons, they studied and collected the strange fish found there – and created this memorable photo diary of their trip.

Las Baulas Leatherback Turtle Conservation Project, Costa Rica at:
http://www.coas.drexel.edu/environ/costa-rica/Las_Baulas/Project/Index.html
Visit one of the few places in the world where leatherback turtles lay their eggs and learn about an important conservation project dedicated to protecting these incredible endangered marine reptiles.

Welcome to Ocean of Know (Sharks) at: http://www.artcontext.com/~ocean/Intro/aintro.html
This website contains lots of terrific information about sharks, including a detailed look at their anatomy and physical features. You'll come away with a new appreciation for these underwater hunters after you plunge into the "Ocean of Know."

ACKNOWLEDGMENTS

What we most enjoy about travelling are the people we meet en route – people who open windows into different cultures, and who teach us about other ways of living and of seeing the world. During our journeys in the Solomon Islands, we have made many friends; it is impossible to name everyone here, and the following list is far from complete, but we are enormously grateful to all the people who have treated us like *wantoks*, welcoming us into their villages and their homes, and helping us in so many ways.

On Santa Isabel Island, we thank Chief James of Kilokaka, John Selwyn and Mr. Johnston of Samasodu, and Edith Ellison and Nurse Stanley of Kia. Also, Christina and Jemima Thagramana and Charles Fox of Kora Islet, and Henry and Joseph of Kukutin, Wagina Island. In Gizo we thank Andrew Simpson of the Gizo Explorer Hotel. In the Gella Islands we thank Paul Jack of Tathi Village. In Marovo Lagoon we thank James and Linethy Kolikeda of Mbili, David and Merver Livingstone Nonga of Chubikopi, Reynold Barora of Nggasini, and John and Oona of Patutiva. In Roviana Lagoon we thank Chief Nathan of Sikele, Gideon Buka, Oliver Green and John Kororo of Baraula, and Likey and Silas of Nusa Hope. In Vonavona Lagoon we thank Tony and Kuria Hughes of Pinadapada, John and Pitu Genu of Mandou and Joe and Lisa Entrikin of the Zipolo Habu Resort, Lola Island. In Munda we thank Mariana and Dave Cooke of Solomon Sea Divers, David Kera and all the staff of the Agnes Lodge, and Ester Gwen of the Sunflower Restaurant.

Special thanks to Joseph Tasker and Basia Patteson, for helping to make our return to the Solomon Islands in 1999/2000 so memorable. In Honiara, we thank Neil Posolo and Joe Gallos of the Solomon Kitano Mendana Hotel for their quiet and kind efficiency, and Patricia and Robert Hans for their warm hospitality.

And to Lillian Murray, Diane and Mark Studley, Gina Stone, Nicholas Lovejoy, Barbara Gordon, Marcia Haller, Katie McKelligott, Michael Adams, Ann and John Tennant, Sarah Pearson, Katie Dodd and Colin Overy, our thanks for having the faith, trust and courage to accompany us on our further explorations of this remote and beautiful part of the world.

We are grateful to Feathercraft for the K2 Expedition kayak that has lasted nine years and thousands of miles, to Cascade Designs for the excellent Seal Line dry bags that have protected our gear and equipment during many expeditions, and to Patagonia for the clothing that still looks stylish after months of exposure to sun, sea and sand.

Our thanks to Rick Wilks for inviting us to share our adventures with a young audience, to Debora Pearson for her enthusiastic co-authorship, to Sheryl Shapiro for her inspired design work and to Carmen Ngai for her lush and lovely maps.

Finally, and as always, our thanks to our mothers, Bee and Justina, for their steadfast love and their prayers when we're so far away.

Maria Coffey and Dag Goering
Munda, Western Province, Solomon Islands
February 14, 2000

Many thanks to Maria Coffey and Dag Goering, for sharing their trip memories with me and introducing me, through their experiences, to the Solomons. Many thanks, as well, to Rick Wilks of Annick Press, who conceived the terrific idea of an adventure travel series for kids, invited me on the unexpected adventure of creating this book, and gave me an opportunity to explore new territory as a writer. Special thanks to Sheryl Shapiro, who displayed much elegance and grace in her work as this book's designer and whose trouble-shooting skills, ever-present sense of humor, and professional manner always fill me with admiration. I also send out my appreciation to Sandra Booth, publishing assistant at Annick, who tracked down the eye-catching turtle photo on page 66-67 and helped me compile the websites section of the book. Thanks, too, to Marg Anne Morrison, also at Annick, who compiled the index and did some last-minute proofreading.

And finally, my work on this book would not have been possible without my husband, Michael, who explained to me how generators and power stations work, listened patiently while I mused out loud, over and over, about life in the Solomons, and who helped lighten my load, as well as my spirits, when the going was rough. I am grateful for his support.

Debora Pearson
Toronto
February 29, 2000

IN THE SAME SERIES:

**52 Days by Camel: My Sahara Adventure
by Lawrie Raskin with Debora Pearson**

**By Truck to the North: My Arctic Adventure
by Andy Turnbull with Debora Pearson**

We dedicate this book to the late Victor Thagramana,
whose laughter and joy in life we will always remember.
—M.C. and D.G.

For the youngest members of the Carmichael families: my great-nieces,
Erica and Geneva, and my great-nephew, Ryan. I hope that each of you
will have many delightful adventures and discover
your heart's desire as you make your way through the world.
—D.P.

Annick Press Ltd.

We acknowledge the support of the Canada Council for the Arts, the Ontario Arts Council, and the Government of
Canada through the Book Publishing Industry Development Program (BPIDP) for our publishing activities.

Cataloging in Publication Data

Coffey, Maria, 1952-
Jungle islands : my South Sea adventure

(Travel adventure books by Annick Press)
ISBN 1-55037-597-0 (bound)
ISBN 1-55037-596-2 (pbk.)

1. Coffey, Maria, 1952- - Journeys – Solomon Islands – Juvenile literature.
2. Goering, Dag – Journeys – Solomon Islands – Juvenile literature.
3. Solomon Islands – Description and travel – Juvenile literature.
4. Sea kayaking – Solomon Islands – Juvenile literature. I. Pearson, Debora. II. Goering, Dag. III. Title. IV. Series.

DU850.C633 2000   j919.59304   C00-930197-6

The text was typeset in Apollo and AGOld face.

Distributed in Canada by:
Firefly Books Ltd.
3680 Victoria Park Avenue
Willowdale, ON
M2H 3K1

Published in the U.S.A. by Annick Press (U.S.) Ltd.
Distributed in the U.S.A. by:
Firefly Books (U.S.) Inc.
P.O. Box 1338
Ellicott Station
Buffalo, NY 14205

Manufactured in China.

Visit us at: **www.annickpress.com**